New Hope® Publishers
P. O. Box 12065
Birmingham, AL 35202-2065
www.newhopepubl.com

Library of Congress Cataloging-in-Publication Data

Smith, Cyncie, 1954-
    The joyful shepherd/written and illustrated by Cyncie Smith.
        p. cm.
    ISBN 1-56309-484-3
    1. Lost sheep (Parable)—Juvenile literature.
  2. Parables. 3. Bible stories—N.T. I. Title.
    BT378.L6 S65 2001
    226.8'09505—dc21

                        00-012387

ISBN: 1-56309-484-3
N018104 • 0501 • 5M1

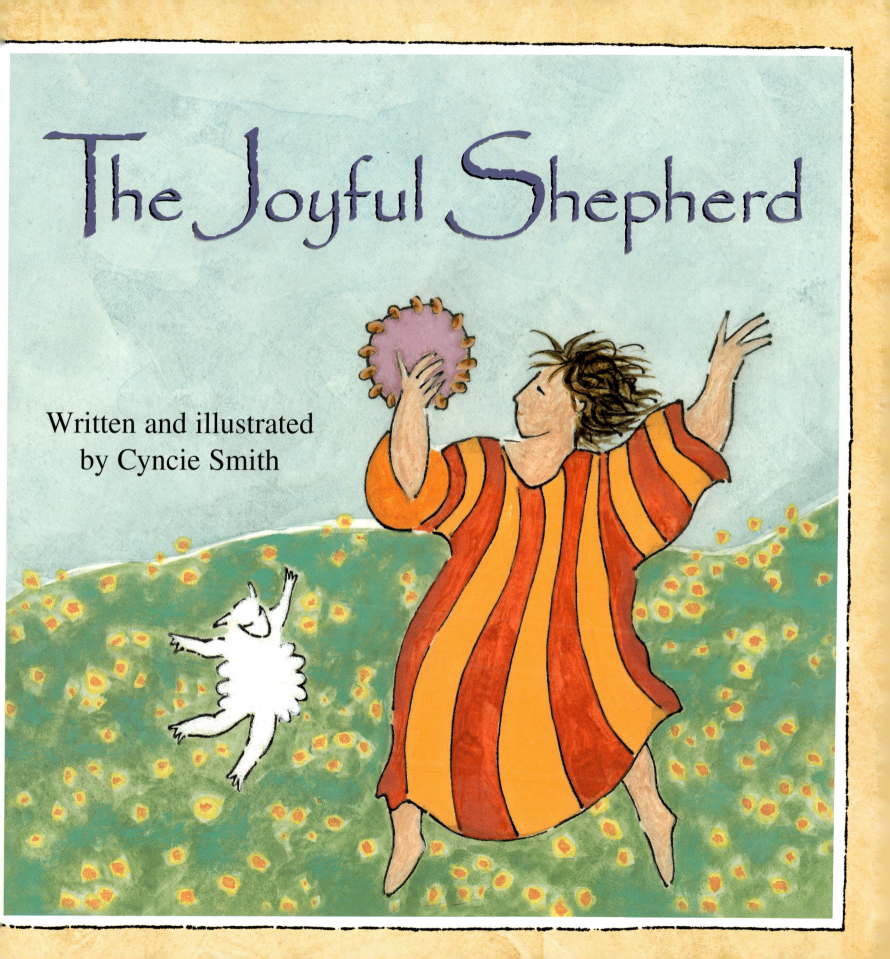

The Joyful Shepherd

Written and illustrated
by Cyncie Smith

Dedication

To my parents
for all their love,
support, and encouragement.

There was a good shepherd

And he had many sheep.

He watched over them as they grazed on the hills.

He guided them into pastures of tender grass.

And he took them to drink from clear, still waters.

His sheep followed him wherever he went—
just like good sheep should,

Except for one,

Who wandered off on his own one day, to eat some extra grass

And to play in the fields a little longer.

But soon it grew dark

For night was coming.

The sky got cloudy and it started to rain.

Then it stormed. The little sheep was frightened.

So frightened that he just started running
and not looking where he was going.

He ran right into a bush full of thorns.
He was stuck and couldn't get out.

In the meantime, the shepherd had gone home
and was putting his sheep to bed

When he noticed that one was missing!

Quickly he ran out into the storm to search for his lost sheep.

He searched every hill, every valley,

And every bush

Until he found his dear little sheep.

He hugged and kissed it, put it on his shoulder,

And went singing and dancing all the way home.

When he returned, the shepherd
called together his friends and neighbors

And had a great, big party

To rejoice over his found sheep.

About the Author

Formerly a children's art teacher, Cyncie Smith has a keen talent for rich and simple illustrations that appeal to both children and adults. Cyncie has studied at the New Orleans Academy of Fine Arts and had several art showings with her mother, also an artist, around the southeast. Her artwork has been featured on an Advent calendar and various greeting cards. *The Joyful Shepherd* is her first book. Cyncie lives in New Orleans with her family.